I0830825

Embrace
Yourself
A journey from subconscious to superconscious
Munit Vikram

Embrace Yourself

Munit Vikram

Touchingchords is about impacting people and their destiny in the best possible manner. It is the endeavor to help people fight their inhibitions and embrace their truer, fuller, complete Self. It is about a journey from past into the future. It is rewiring the thoughts to revamp the behaviour and eventually to change lives.

Munit Vikram
Gurgaon, Haryana, India
www.touchingchords.com

Start your journey to know yourself and embrace yourself

CONTENTS

To my parents ,

Mr R R Yadav and Mrs Vimla Yadav

Acknowledgements

My journey into writing began couple of years ago through blogs and with time it took the form of a book. The pandemic which jostled the world, gave me time to reflect on the passion which somehow took the backseat back then. I was finally able to find time to talk about things that matters to me, things that affects me and things that when worked upon can do wonders. With this book my endeavor is to provide self-help to all those who need a change. It is for all those people who needs to empower themselves and be a better version of themselves.

This book would not have seen the light of the day, if it had not been some important people influencing me all throughout.I would take some time to thank and acknowledge those people. My parents Mr R R Yadav and Mrs Vimla Yadav, for being the incredible support and faith that they have in me. Thanks Ma & Pa. My sisters, Anit and Viragya for continuously motivating me and giving brutal feedback - every time. My friend & mentor - Raja, for inspiring me and keeping me on toes. I would also like to thank pixabay, whose pictures have been a boon to me. Lastly, thanks to all my friends and family (could not list down the names) to be a part of my journey. Will conclude with, this is the beginning...

Prologue

What started as a weekly Blog, on self-help, quickly grew into a series of   articles, dealign with various topics from knowing yourself to knowing others. It helps to deal with the outside world without compromising on your core set of values. We bring forth this book for you to carry it along, read and ponder over. Knowing yourself is a journey.

Chapter 1

"Four Levels of Consciousness"

We have all gone through the childhood phase, creating memories and then carrying them along. This is a phase where a child gets to know himself and the world around. It is a crucial time as it lays the foundation of your character by your experiences and the choice that you make. Consciously or subconsciously we choose the level that we want to operate in life. There are four levels of consciousness that one operates our of know, awareness is the key.

Level 1 - Life Happens To Me
The first conscious level is the belief that Life Happens To Me. It is the most convenient and comfortable level to be in. Mostly people choose this state as it helps them to shirk of their responsibility.They have always, anything or everything to be blamed for the things that go wrong. They fondly play the victim card all through their life and benefit out of people.They can be easily spotted narrating, how things have been so rough for them and blaming destiny if not people or circumstances.We should be very careful of such people as their intention is always tainted and for purely their personal benefit. It is very likely that operating at this level of conscious, muddles the integrity with intent.

Level 2 - Life Happens For Me
The second conscious level is believing that Life Happens For Me. People in this state are the ones who take responsibility

of their actions. They believe that whatever is happening to them or with them is inherently associated to their actions in someway or the other.This helps them to retrospect and more often then not they are able to rectify it. It is good to be responsible for your actions but what is more important is to be aware of this trait. It is because of their innate habit of being responsible that they are pushed into taking the blame for other's mistake.They are easily manipulated into playing the scapegoat.

Level 3 - Life Happens Through Me

The third conscious level is the belief that Life Happens Through Me. This is an evolved state to be in. Usually and largely people fall in the first two levels of conscious. People operating in third level of conscious state are the ones who are the anchor with the cause. They are heavily guided by their goals in life.They firmly believe that life has more to offer and they deserve that more. This drives them to break the stereotypes and create history. It is not a cakewalk to be in, it requires tremendous hard work, lot of dedication, constant motivation and an undying urge of creating your own brandname.People in this state doesn't dabble between playing victim or accepting the life that is as it is. They challenge themselves and end-up empowering themselves.

Level 4 - Life Happens As Me

The fourth conscious level is believing that Life Happens As Me. This is a super evolved state to be in. People operating in this level of conscious are the ones who are guided by the bigger cause a calling that changes them for good. They are the ones who knows that their life on earth is with a mission which is much higher in magnitude. They are not bonded by the association or dissociation of the world but are connected with the supreme force.

Every individual should thrive to move on from the level of conscious they are in to the next one rather being trapped in one level all through their life. On another philosophical note the lifecycle of a human has all the four levels of conscious. The childhood state is the `first level of conscious, the teen phase is the second level of conscious, the adult is the third level of conscious and the old age is the fourth level of conscious.It is imperative as the role, responsibilities and the expectations we have at different stages of life resonates cohesively with the levels.

Chapter 2

"Five Types of Personalities"

In our day to day life , personal and professional we come across different personalities and with some we get along well while others are constantly on our back. Ever wondered, why some people are difficult and some indifferent and very few nice to be with.

Well the different personalities that an individual has, it is the manifestation of their emotions, physiology, feelings and thought process. This is beautifully captured in SATIR Communication Model. The model categorizes the human personalities into five buckets. Knowing the categorization makes it easy to accept different personalities and assists to build a defense mechanism which will hold against falling prey. Here are the five personality types:

Type 1: Blamer
The first one, which is very common is the blamer. I will not be wrong if `i say that larger population falls under this category. They are in a habit of blaming others for everything that is going wrong for them or with them. They never take responsibility for their actions and find a scapegoat. The loudest person around showing off to be working hard but complaining of lack of support is the Blamer. Hardly they can be seen taking responsibility of the action going wrong and standing for others. Beware of such individuals, they are menace to a team and toxic as high manipulative they singlehandedly destroy the culture.

Type 1: Placater

The non assertive individual who does not have an opinion and says yes to the majority is the Placater. They are the ones with no opinion and want to be in the comfortable zone. No opinions, no questions and going with the flow. They are easy to be identified. They need to be challenged so locate them in your team and push them with the facts. They look for the godfathers to comply by and for easy survival.

Type 3: Computer

Computer are the third category, who do not display emotions and involve themselves socially. They are mostly task oriented and practical. For them it is work devoid of hoopla and deep down they have a sense of fairness. These are the few people who will work but will expect others also to do their job. They can be identified easily as they are do as directed but can be easily maneuvered. They need direction and mentoring.

Type 4: Distracter

Fourth category are the ones who have distracted themselves from the deep hurt, loss or heavy emotion and have found new avenue to channelize their energy. They are very passionate in their work as that is the way they have chosen to focus their energy to. They are the ones working on the projects and ensuring it is completed. They feel emotionally connected with their place of work and their work. They are very hardworking but at the same time aggressive. They ensure success. The easiest way to lose them is to doubt them. Their build up emotion on being doubted at will propel them to detach and move on.

Type 5: Leveller

The last category are the levellers. They are emotionally balanced , focused and the stable type. Hard feat to achieve so very few fall under this category. They are the ones with few words and lot of action. Their focus is always he bigger picture. They can be easily identified as they are the ones who are the leaders in the group. They let others to be the manager and win it by leading it to completion.

If you are able to identify the people around you basis this model then it will help you to deal with them in a constructive way. You will not fall victim to their outer persona which is very misleading. Gone are the days ,when you got what you saw. Now every personality depicts the Iceberg model. So, being informed is the only weapon that we have, to deal with situations and people.

Chapter 3

" Your Learning Styles "

Learning is a continuous process and as rightly said **" you stop learning when you stop breathing"**. It becomes imperative for all of us to know our learning styles to make the process optimally benefitted. Once we identify our learning pattern we can always use it to teach people around, personally and professionally. Each one of us should deliberate on their learning pattern so that it becomes beneficial for the one who is learning and also for the one who is teaching.

The **VAK model** predominantly used, is to identify the learning style of an individual was developed by Walter Burke Barbe. It primarily focusses on three sensory receptors Visual (eyes), Auditory (ears) and Kinaesthetic (touch) to absorb the information. He boiled it down to the fact that any information is received by eyes, ears or touch and use of either of it is heightened in every human being. Since all of us has a distinctive way of learning so we fit in the VAK model.

Visual Learners are the ones who are heavily dependent on their visual sensory for their learning of all form. For them it becomes easy to grasp any info if it is visually displayed. They remember faces but not names.They can be easily identified by various characteristics as they are distracted during lectures, seminars unless it is a pictorial representation. They have to picture things to remember it. They are usually good with spellings. They are the ones who usually talks fast.

They are usually well organized and doesn't understand directions when told. Map comes easy to them than directions. They remember charts / diagrams / movie scene in detail or graphic details of an incident and present them distinctively. You cannot help noticing their use of you see, it looks, it views etc.

Auditory Learners have to hear or speak to learn things. They are good with lectures and responds well to directions. They remember names, numbers but miss on face or color. They have to say things to themselves or repeat to themselves to remember it. They feel that their concentration is high when they listen to music and read/ write. They never miss on the tone of the speaker and it stays with them.

They usually perform well in oral and are good listeners. They remember the lectures, dialogues and can present them after years. The use of phrases I hear you, it sounds like and easily get distracted by faintest sound. They are the ones who are rhythmic in their speech.

Kinaesthetic Learners respond to sense of touch or movement. They learn best when they experience through touch or in motion.They can be easily spotted randomly touching things in the store. They will use their hands often while describing. While memorizing or cramming , they will pace speedily. When they have to think deeply that's when they would prefer to go for a walk or will be in any form of movement. Usually draw or doodle to grasp things.

To remember things they write instead of typing. To teach them, use of on the job training, simulation, work experience or any form of physical activity gets best results. They are the ones who are usually soft in tone and slow while talking. They are easily identified by their habit of touching or holding things to memorize it. They are usually restless in a room and cannot go unnoticed.

Chapter 4

"Responsiveness Is The Differentiator"

Ever wondered what makes a person successful at times and a failure at other times. Why is it, when we look back and say, it would have been different if I would have chosen A over B. Would it have actually made a difference? well the answer is YES. It is your decision which makes the difference. It is your ability to react positively or negatively to a situation or an event that makes it a success or a failure. So it is imperative that picking A over B changes your life in entirety.

Apparently it becomes important to understand the dynamics behind it. The decision making involves the complex nerves in our brain which is primarily bifurcated into two hemispheres, the left hemisphere and the right hemisphere. The left hemisphere controls the right side of your body and is responsible for all the logic, rationale and practicality. Whereas the right hemisphere controls the left side of the body and is responsible for the emotions, creativity and art.

Every human being is directed by either of the hemisphere, inclining a person to be logical or emotional in their approach. So a person with the active right hemisphere tends to be emotional eventually making all the decisions with emotions. On the contrary the left hemisphere individual will be more logical in their decisions. However whatever the situation be, using either of the approach is not recommended. The reason being they cloud your judgement. Carl Sagan's words **" where we have strong emotions, we're liable to fool ourselves"** says it all. More often than ever, decisions made in emotion largely backfires specially if it involves your career, business or financial matters. It should be dealt with objectivity or rationally. For instance you accept an offer because the hiring manager made you feel good or is your friend will make you pay dearly in the long run. Unless you have evaluated the offer and weighed the options with the facts , you should not accept it. On the contrary emotions should rule the decision making when it has to do with love, friendship or a feeling. Making friends after evaluating the value they bring to the table or how will they benefit to you in a long run ,will give you a partner not a friend.

However the ideal decision making technique is in between the emotion and logic and that is to decide with an Informed or an intelligent mind. As recommended, all decisions should be made with the intelligent mind which is a combination of logic, emotion and a controlled you. Now that is called a real challenge to do in a real life. Why? Reacting to a person , situation or an event on your reflex is a natural way. But to step back , detach yourself from the situation and then use both the faculties (emotion and logic) in making a decision is a task. This acumen comes with lot of practice and experience. It is highly recommended that the decisions that are crucial to your life, the ones that will impact you , your near and dear ones should be taken with an intelligent mind.

Chapter 5

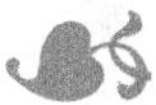

"What Drives Our Behaviour"

Human Behaviour is steered through motives. Motive is the driving force that motivates us all through our lives varying as per the different stages that we are in. According to humanist psychologist Abraham Maslow, our actions are motivated in order to achieve certain needs.Maslow first introduced this concept of a hierarchy of needs in his 1943 paper "A Theory of Human Motivation" and his subsequent book Motivation and Personality.His hierarchy of needs comprise of a five-tier model of human needs, often depicted as hierarchical levels within a pyramid. The five tier model is

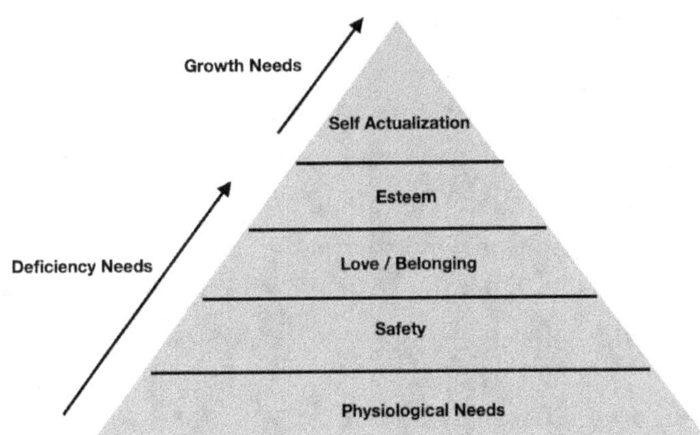

a pyramid of needs in an order that can be further bifurcated into deficiency needs and growth needs.

In the bottom of the pyramid is the **Physiological needs.** These are our basic needs such as food, water, shelter, homeostasis etc. These core basic needs drive us for sustenance and are pivotal to our survival. Our physiological needs are universal and must be met first. This means that if a human is struggling to meet their physiological needs, then they are unlikely to intrinsically pursue other needs which are safety, belongingness, esteem, and self-actualization in the model. Not able to meet the basic needs creates displeasure and affects the behaviour.

It's only when we are able to satisfy the basic needs that we intrinsically pursue the higher needs which is **Safety & Security.** At this level, the needs for security and safety become primary.Safety, or security needs, relate to a person's need to feel safe and secure in their life and surroundings. These needs manifest themselves in ways such as a preference for job security, insurance policies, disability accommodations, etc. Having to meet the need helps an individual to enhance their self worth.

The third level in Maslow's needs model is the **Social Needs** which entails emotions such as love, belonginess or intimacy. He further elucidated that this level of the hierarchy outlines the need for friendship, intimacy, family, and love. Humans have the need to give and receive love; to feel like they belong in a group. When deprived of these needs, individuals may experience loneliness or depression which impacts their behaviour and eventually their personality.

At the fourth level in Maslow's hierarchy is the innate need for appreciation and recognition. When the needs at the bottom levels have been satisfied then the **Esteem Needs** start to play a more prominent role in motivating behavior.Those who lack self-esteem and the respect of others can develop feelings of inferiority.Maslow further broke up esteem needs into two categories: the need for respect from others and the need for respect from oneself. Respect from others relates to achieving fame, prestige, and recognition. Respect from oneself relates to dignity, confidence, competence, independence, and freedom.

At the peak of Maslow's hierarchy are the **Self-actualization needs**. "What a man can be, he must be" This adage forms the basis of the perceived need for self-actualization.To satisfy this level of need, a person must not only fulfill in the previous needs but master them.To understand this level of need, a person must not only succeed in the previous needs but master them.The need for self-actualization can manifest in different ways, such as acquiring skills or seeking happiness which os more inclined towards personal growth than worrying about others opinion.

Consequently the striking difference between two bifurcations of the model, growth and deficiency needs is the change in motivation as needs are met. For instance, motivation increases as growth needs are met however motivation decreases as deficiency needs are met. However a more evolved perspective is that these levels overlap. Even if a person reaches higher levels, their motivation is directed more towards these levels but they will still continue to pursue lower levels of the hierarchy but with less intensity.

Understanding the Maslow's model, explains the human behaviour. But it also provides an insight, that not meeting the needs does not make an individual a less of an achiever. If you are not able to meet the deficiency needs it should not stop you to aim for the growth needs. As a human, we all have an innate desire or we are naturally wired to meet the self actualization needs. That should be our motivator.

Chapter 6

"Finding Scapegoat For Everything...
Beware!!!"

A regular site nowadays, is to find yourself amidst people who never take responsibility of their actions. They would have anything or anyone to blame, instead of themselves.Project did not meet the deadline because I got the report late, laden with errors; I am late to work because there was congestion on the road; I ended up with the wrong guy (even after dating him for seven years) because he duped me into.This is how the locust of responsibility is

conveniently transferred to others. On the onset it feels usual and can be substantiated, that I am merely stating the facts but it is a serious distorted defense mechanism developed in the course of time to safeguard personal interests. In

Projection was conceptualized b Sigmund Freud and eventually refined by K Abraham and Anna Freud.

According to Sigmund, projection refers to unconsciously taking unwanted emotions or traits you don't like about yourself and attributing them to someone else or placing it to the outside world. Projection, one main mechanism of paranoia, is an innate part of narcissistic and borderline personalities.As it is an Ego defense mechanism, it is primarily practiced with fragile ego individuals or people who have low self esteem and inferiority complex. As a matter of fact, humans tend to feel more comfortable seeing negative qualities in others rather than in themselves and that can be an answer to that Projection is now practiced extensively bu the groups or society as a whole. Projection can be of three different forms

Neurotic Projection – This is a defense mechanism where unwanted thoughts, motivations, desires, and feelings that cannot be accepted as one's own are attributed to someone else. For instance, if you don't like a colleague at work then you would tell people that he doesn't likes you.

Complementary Projection – This occurs when individuals assume that others feel the same way they do. For instance, If I am an opportunist then I will believe that everyone out there is an opportunist and it is ok to be one.

Complimentary Projection – It is the assumption that other people can do the same things as well as oneself. For instance, If I am good with detailing then m assumption is that everyone is good with it.

The projection can be positive or negative and does not take place arbitrarily, but rather seized on and exaggerated an element that already exists on a small scale in the person.

Melanie Klein, one of the founding figures of psychoanalytic theory who furthered Freud's theories, pointed out that projection is not just about denying feelings or emotions of ourselves but also about connecting ourselves to others in a way that allows us to feel we can acquire parts of what they have.

This is captured within positive projection. For example, if you project your ability to be powerful onto another who happens to be very successful then it might be that you are unconsciously trying to attach yourself to their success. If exaggerated then you begin to take the credit fo other's work without feeling an iota of guilt. Additionally, people who project ado more damage to self than others. They never learn and grow as all their life the have shirked away from taking responsibility. More often than not they lose on relationships and in the long run get sidelined.

Now, If you recognize yourself as someone who projects or being told as that you project, there's no need to beat yourself up about it. This can just lead to more projecting. Instead, try to focus on why you're projecting.

There are a few ways to go about deciphering it. Firstly be honest with yourself and acknowledge that you project and then delve deeper to understand the reason behind it. It can be related to the repressed emotions from childhood or a behaviour you might have witnessed around which unknowingly got emulated and later became the trait. Secondly you might want to discuss it with someone who knows you better and is reasonable. Lastly you may seek help from a therapist. Remember, only when we get rid of projecting ourselves on others, that we are able to discover our self.And discovering oneself brings back the true identity which strengthens the self worth.

Chapter 7

"Eye Accessing Cues : Know Your People"

According to Maslow's Hierarchy, as elucidated in my previous post, one of the needs is social needs. Social needs obligate an individual to interact with each other, which can be in a variety of forms. It becomes imperative for all of us to not just comprehend the communication style but absorb the cues alongside which talk volumes. It abets us in taking our understanding of another person to a next level which can benefit the association. It is famously called as **Eye Accessing Cues.**

This concept in NLP, can be expressed as an automatic, unconscious eye movements usually accompany particular thought processes, and indicate the access and use of particular representational systems. For instance it can actually be deciphered, how an individual is thinking with the **Eye Accessing Cues (EAQ)** . it is not a mandate to be taken as a gospel truth but if practiced enough can provide some surprising outcomes. We all are receptive to any one form while we absorb information. It can either be through Auditory, Visual or Kinesthetics. EAQ indicate whether a person is thinking in images, sounds, self talk or through their feelings.

Ans per the EAQ theory, while you direct a question to an individual he /she most often then not will move his/her eyes either to the left side or to the right side.If the eyes move to the left side then the information is constructed or made up. However if the eyes moves to the right side then the information provided is the remembered one. Now following the eyes movements require practice as some people are too good at maneuvering. Another important thing, this left and right representation varies if the person is left handed. So there are primarily six representations from the eye movements as stated below.

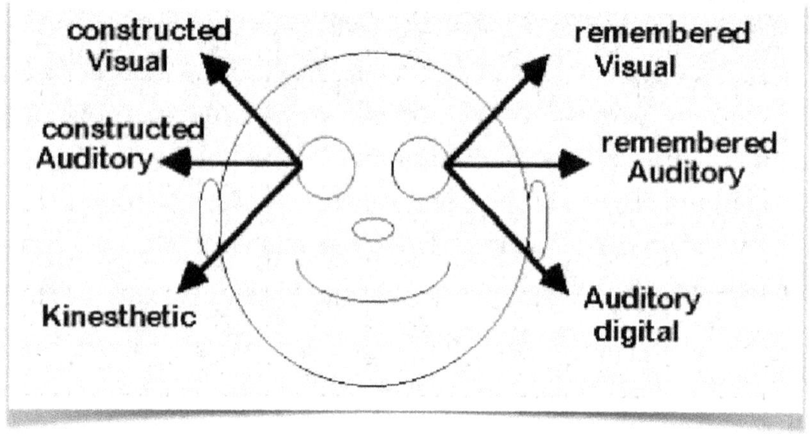

- **Visual Constructed (VC), eyes move to the left-upper corner.**

- **Visual Remembered (VR), eyes move to the right-upper corner.**

- **Audio Constructed (AC), eyes move horizontally to the left.**

- **Audio Remembered (AR), eves move horizontally to the right.**

- **Feelings (K) and body sensations, eyes move to the lower left.**

- **Internal Dialogue (AD), eyes move to the lower right.**

While we all have extensive experiences, which eventually takes the form of memories. The memories of all the experiences, are stored as an internal representation. Each specific event is kept in the brain a s a picture, sound, feeling, or thought.In fact, all of our memories are stored as a specific set of images, slides, movies, sounds, feelings, smells, and tastes. This is how we make a difference between one set of memories from another. We mentally recreate and recall our experiences (memories) with these stored pictures, words, sounds, and physical feelings as we think.

It is believed that eye – nerve is the one closest to the brain and that is the reason it gives away when posed with a question. Now for instance, if you hurl a question to someone , What was the colour of your first vehicle ? or what all flowers you had in your garden ? To answer these, if the person is moving his eyes to the right then he is trying to remember or retrieving the image stored whereas if the person moves the eyes to the left then he is trying to construct or make up the image. Similarly it holds true, if the question is about sound, feel, smell or taste. It is indeed an interesting concept and I remember trying it to each one that i spoke to when I first learnt about it.As mentioned above the eye moves towards the upper/middle/lower of left side or right side.

Not only as an NLP practitioner but as an individual I am convinced, that this is an extremely helpful technique if used judiciously, along with the monitoring of the tone, body posture, breathing and hand movements. It helps to understand someone's thinking style, thought process and establish rapport. It gives you a preview about the other person, as the old adage goes " **eyes are the windows of the soul**" it is in more than one ways.

Chapter 8

"Are You Around A Narcissistic ?"

While the world together, is dealing with major crisis's such as pandemic, recession, natural calamity it becomes imperative for all of us that we stay strong at an individual level and in no circumstance should succumb to it. This is a herculean task as these situations test and challenge our mental capacity. Now, some of us can manage these adverse conditions perfectly well, whereas the remaining half finds it impossible to even imagine being the victim of it let alone endure it. The premise to such bifurcation is the Personality that we have, or it would be right to say Personality Disorder.

Then what is personality? An individual's personality is what defines how they perceive the world around them. It is a range of characteristics and features that cause them to think, feel, and act in a particular way in any given circumstances. In addition to it, the background, environment, genes all these factors contribute in shaping the personality.

Now Personality Disorder is a condition with an individual, where he has challenge in responding to stressful and difficult situations and in turn getting himself totally consumed by the demands of life. This impacts there wellbeing, people around them and all their relationships in every aspect. These experiences can lead to distress and social isolation and increase the risk of depression and other mental health issues.

Personality Disorder has been classified into ten types which are further categorized as three clusters. They are

Cluster A (Odd, bizarre, eccentric)
- Paranoid (PPD)
- Schizoid (SiPD)
- Schizotypal (SyPD)

Cluster B (Dramatic, erratic)
- Antisocial (AnPD)
- Borderline (BPD)
- Histrionic (HPD)
- Narcissistic (NPD)

Cluster C (Anxious, fearful)
- Avoidant (AvPD)
- Dependent (DPD)
- Obsessive-compulsive (OPD)

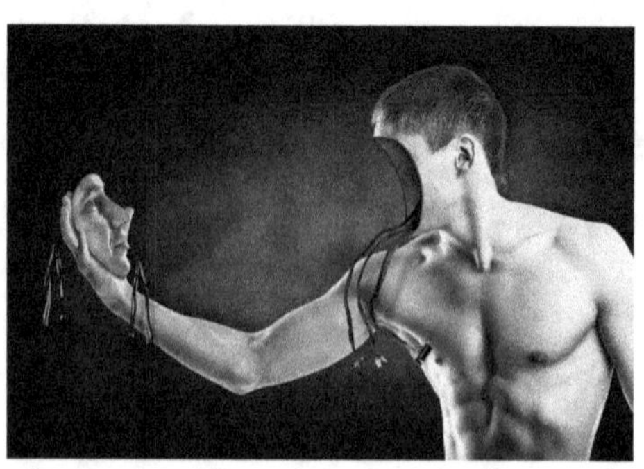

Narcissistic Personality Disorder (NPD) is the most common disorder and therefore needs to be talked about at first, eventually shall be elucidating each of the personality disorder in my subsequent blogs. Narcissism concept was coined by Sigmund Freud in 1914. He explains NPD as closely associated with egocentrism, a personality characteristic in which people see themselves and their interests and opinions as the only ones that really matter. They have close to zero interest in others and lack empathy, moreover they are unable to feel or appreciate feelings that are not their own. The hallmarks of narcissistic personality disorder (NPD) are grandiosity, a lack of empathy for other people, and a need for admiration.

People with this condition are frequently described as arrogant, self-centered, manipulative, and demanding. They are envious of others and expects them to be the same of themselves. They manipulate and readily lies and exploits others to achieve their aims. Most likely they are easily stung by criticism or defeat and react with disdain or anger but social withdrawal or the false appearance of humility follows. They can be easily identified as someone with grandiose self-admiration and lack of empathy for others. Always striving for their benefits while exploiting anyone they come across. If they feel they are obstructed, then they will not shy away from taking serious revenge which in most cases has disastrous consequences to everyone involved.

Narcissists are constantly comparing themselves to others, especially successful people, which can trigger feelings of envy. They never shy away from creating rumors to malign someone and will go lengths to destroy someone if they feel threatened by them. And if they achieve success in their lives, they have this inherent belief that everyone is envious of them. They are never contented and that is the reason they are seldom happy with life.

This is a serious disorder and needs to be treated, unfortunately NPD's never realize or reflect it as a distortion.

Psychotherapy is recommended for the disorder, however if you happen to come across some narcissist at workplace, it is best to steer away and avoid getting into arguments. They always have the last word and if not, then they ensure it gets ugly with tactics and manipulation. If you have someone with NPD in your personal circle, then it is recommended to set boundaries and be assertive on day to day issues. To sum it up, the emotional and physical impact of working with or living with a person with NPD can be severe. It is extremely taxing and will drain you of your mental capacity. Woefully, we don't have much options to help them with the disorder unless they agree to see a therapist.

Chapter 9

"Borderline Personality Disorder (BPD)"

In continuation to the previous chapter about personality disorder, Borderline Personality Disorder is next in line.The name borderline is coined, for its very nature of being sandwiched in between the two ailments 'psychoses' and 'neuroses'. Historically, all the mental conditions were classified in either of the two categories. BPD is famously known as **Emotionally Unstable Personality Disorder.**

As the name indicates, individual with persistent severe emotional imbalance who have immense challenge in regulating their emotions define the category.

So how do we identify BPD in individuals? Usually people with borderline personality disorder may experience intense interludes of anger, depression, and anxiety that can last from a few hours to days. Additionally, lacking to regulate the emotions, lead to impulsivity, poor self-image, stormy relationships and intense emotional responses to stressors.The condition is strongly manifested in seven different forms.

a) **Impulsive, Self Destructive Behaviour** – People with BPD usually respond to stressor with instant gratifying acts. That may be, impulsively spend money you don't have, binge eat, drive recklessly, engage in shoplift, or overdo it with drugs or alcohol. However if these actions help in uplifting your moods, every now and then , it is not a disorder.

b) **Intense Fear Of Abandonment And Feeling Of Emptiness.**- BPD's have a constant belief of people abandoning them and this belief turns into fear which demands them to behave irrationally. They start to implement desperate measures to hold them in their lives with Begging, clinging and stalking them to the extent that they turn their back on. Additionally they also have this chronic feeling of void in themselves which leads to doing drugs, food binge or meaningless relationships.

c) **Distorted Self Image** – They have trouble in sticking to opinions about themselves and others which affects moods, values, opinions, goals and relationships.This might be the reason that they frequently juggle between jobs, relationships, places and faith.

d) **Unstable Relationships** – People with the condition, often land themselves dwindling in between idealization and devaluation. It is irrational to love someone immensely and at the second instance you disdain them. BPD's tend to be intense in their relationships but loose on them quickly because of this constant swings in between idealization and devaluation.

e) Self Inflicted Behaviour – People with BPD have this tendency of inflicting pain to themselves. They are prone to suicides leading to death or can wound themselves or even cut or burn themselves in the wake of self destruction. This self harm is exacerbated with emotional outburst.

f) Explosive Anger – They loose their temper on the spur of the moment and the magnitude of this rage is huge which can range in between verbal outbursts to violent behaviour out of proportion.This is not always directed outwards but at times inward as well.It is these bouts of rage that leads to action so severe that can not be rescind.

g) Dissociative Behaviour – People with BPD condition under stress either become highly suspicious of others or experience unusual feelings of being detached from their own emotions, body or surroundings.

These symptoms of Borderline Personality Disorder do not appear together but in the combination of them and can be triggered by seemingly ordinary events. For instance, feeling of abandonment or emptiness can be triggered bu as trivial as your loved one coming home late. BPD can be owed to many factors such as hereditary, traumatic experience from childhood or setbacks. In most cases brain function is also considered as probable reason as the lack of regulation of the emotions causes BPD.

Like any other disorder, BPD too can be treated as the whole premise is based on the fact that, the personality is the amalgamation of your thoughts, feelings, behaviors for a period of time.Hence changing thoughts, feelings, behaviors will eventually change your personality.

We can start with learning to control the impulse behaviour or practicing being calm in stressful situations. We can engage ourselves with activities that appeases our being. We can bring discipline in our lives with introducing mediation, exercise, proper sleep and healthy diet.

These are baby steps to begin with however if the problem persists then seeking a psychotherapists will be the best bet. Dialectical behavioral therapy (DBT), cognitive behavioral therapy (CBT) and psychodynamic psychotherapy works for people suffering from BPD. Under severe conditions medication is administered.

Like intimated, personality disorders can be treated bu merely acknowledging the problem and working on your behaviour. It is only when it is ignored that it takes the form of a disorder.

As rightly stated, **"Emotions are temporary states of mind ; Don't let them permanently destroy you"**

Chapter 10

"Trust – You Earn It..."

"Trust takes years to build, seconds to break and forever to repair" talks volumes about trust. It is the foundation of every relationship developed in professional or personal capacity. The level of trust, defines the degree of intimacy in a relationship. It is an essence of any relationship. As rightly said "to be trusted is a greater compliment than being loved" since love happens but trust is earned.

Here I am digressing from my Personality Disorder Series posts, only to demystify trust. I strongly   felt the need, because of the personal chats, personal videos, call records doing the rounds. It's kind of become the norm to record calls without the knowledge of the other party. Which does not gives you an edge but questions your integrity and credibility.To make it worse, we are building the culture of distrust.Once we step on to this journey of distrust, then it will not be limited to outsiders but will seep in to your personal territory and will damage it for good. There are three levels of trust that we meddle with basis the connections the we have.

- **Rule Based Trust**– Rule based trust is to la down the ground rules for the connect or relationship, so that neither of the party can take advantage of other. This can be in the form of contract, laws, polices or procedures. It is deemed important for both the parties to stand their sides of the rules. Rules based trust is binding and usually have repercussions if faltered.

- **Knowledge Based Trust** – This level of trust is usually developed after knowing the other person for some time. It is the knowledge garnered in the process of time that warrants a person to establish the Knowledge based trust. This is usually displayed and maintained in the professional environment.

- **Identity Based Trust** – The third level of trust is the highest level of trust that a person places in another person in the passage of time. It indicates that they have shared their hopes, ambitions, success, failure and vulnerability with each other and have proven to keep it uptight. Identity based trust is for personal relationships which are intimate in nature.

The beauty of the level of trust is that it indicates the health of the relationship. For instance, if the intimate relationships are governed bu the Rule based trust, then it's time to ponder. Similarly if you manifest the Identity based trust in the workplace, you are doomed.

So how does the trust develop ? Is it just the gut feeling or a well defined process? To discern it, we shall have to delve

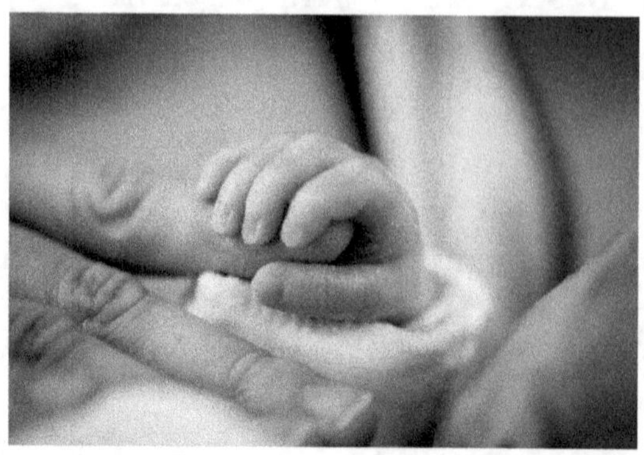

deeper and break down the trust into pieces; symbolically, but that's too higher a price to pay. Trust is a process and we can conveniently chalk out a framework for it. There are five stages to it.

1. **Attraction** – Of all the people we come across, we usually have some vibes about them and that's what associates or dissociates the relatedness.To some we feel attracted to and inherently gets ushered towards them.This is the first stage of trust.

2. **Evaluation** – Can I trust you ? What all can I trust you for ? This is the second stage where we unconsciously start observing the person to base our trust.We are very cautious at this second stage and must say guarded.We weigh each information before we can trust the person with it. This is a critical stage which will lay the foundation of the relationship.

3. **Credibility** – If the second stage is through, that means the opening up starts but still guarded. At this phase, we look for credibility which is an extension to evaluation with more concrete evidence.The more

deeper connection initiates from here as trusting is a delicate process and requires lot of time and patience.

4. **Reliability** – Next stage is the reliability or consistency.Trust gets to take a form if the consistency is maintained. The connect gets profound if we find the consistency in words and actions aligned.This stage requires perseverance and getting to this stage binds the relationship.

5. **Intimacy** – The last stage is the level of intimacy to be decided in unsaid agreement. The premise would be the culmination of stages from one to four. If it has to be friendship, acquaintance, relationship or matrimony is defined.

Once the level of intimacy is decided then it is the commitment to uphold it. It is when this commitment wagers that the trust goes back to the stage two and would need more efforts to root in.

Maintaining trust is not difficult as captured bu **Johnny Cash in his popular single, I Walk The Line.**

Chapter 11

" Know Yourself – Antisocial Personality Disorder "

A sombre meeting turns into a violent one with a haughty boss rebuking the team, is a common site, however the ingrained pattern of this reckless behaviour can lead into a personality disorder if not checked on time. Another category under dramatic personality disorder is **Antisocial Personality Disorder (APD).** The behaviour attributed to this mental condition is the ingrained behavioral display of impulsive, irresponsible and often criminal behaviour. Intrinsically they are manipulative, deceitful , reckless with no consideration to other's sentiments. Characteristically, they are often seen defying the norms, rules, policies or law in general which makes them a lawbreaker.

Like other types of personality disorder, antisocial personality disorder is on a gamut, meaning it ranges in severity from occasional bad behaviour to repeatedly breaking the law and committing serious crimes. APD is more prevalent in men than women. Statistics proves that people with criminal records have high probability, of them suffering with APD's. People with antisocial personality disorder violates any form of rule and would adhere to them only if they are threatened with punishment. They have a tendency to exploit others hence take advantage of them, and feel indifferent toward or even contemptuous of their victims.They understand the emotions of others only to get their ways with them or use the knowledge of others' weaknesses to gain favors or to manipulate an outcome to their personal advantage. Owing to which they rarely are in committed relationships and if they end up with someone then it is laced with abuse, and violence.

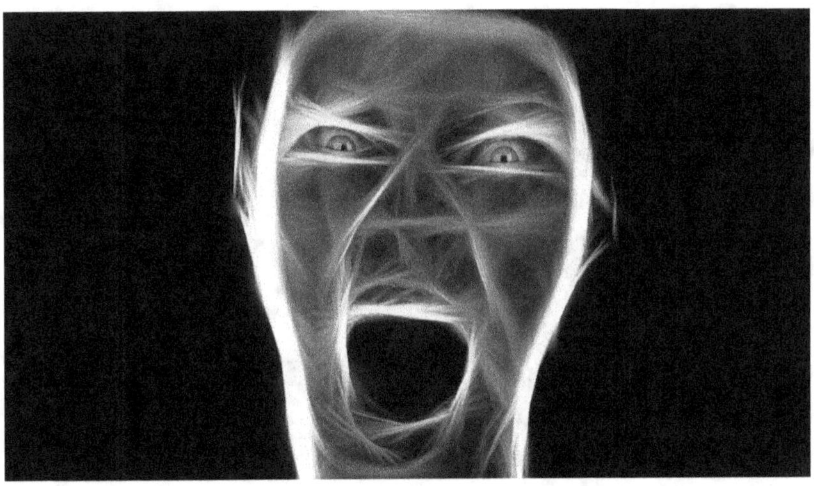

It is believed that childhood abuse, neglect, traumatic childhood experience and even heredity/genes could be the reason behind people developing the antisocial personality disorder. The intermittent outburst, truancy, insensitive toward others magnifies into serious criminal activity, drugs, alcoholism or imprisonment. The alcohol and drug abuse common among people with antisocial personality disorder can exacerbate symptoms of the disorder. When substance abuse and antisocial personality disorder coexist, treatment is more complicated for both.

Consequently APD's have high odds of committing suicide or die prematurely.

Evidence suggests behaviour can improve over time with therapy, even if core characteristics such as lack of empathy remain. But antisocial personality disorder is one of the most difficult types of personality disorders to treat. Though there is huge reluctance of APD's taking treatments but therapy seems to be promising and the best bet in such cases. If the ailment exacerbates then medication is recommended.

We cannot control the ailment at the onset however we can reduce the impact bai being mindful of our behaviour and being in constant touch with yourself. We need to cut out sometime for introspection and practicing being in control. You can do this by practicing relaxation techniques such as deep breathing, meditation, rhythmic exercise, yoga, or tai chi.Concluding with famous adage of Swami Vivekanand – **"Talk to yourself at least once in a day, otherwise you may miss a meeting with an excellent person in the world"**.

Chapter 12

"Histrionic Personality Disorder"

Another category under dramatic personality disorder is **Histrionic Personality Disorder (HPD).** Behavioral pattern that is deeply ingrained with extreme emotionality and attention-seeking behavior is what defines HPD. HPD's are believed to be less lethal than other personality disorders, however they are instrumental in creating a toxic environment if not addressed on time.

Ever came across an individual who evades difficult questions/situations with blatant display of excessive emotion? For instance, coming late to work and when questioned " I had a flat tyre, had to miss breakfast and ma pet is sick".Instantly you would be concerned with any of the above and not in the reason anymore. Similarly you hurl any questions to them and the outcome is destined to be an emotional anecdote which clouds the agenda.

Nurtured with the low self esteem, HPD's create a distorted self image. They base their self esteem on the approval of others which nudges them to constantly seek attention. Their innate behaviour exhibit's excessive emotionality, a tendency to regard things in an emotional manner. People with the condition are uncomfortable or feel unappreciated when they are not the center of attention and most likely resort to dramatic, inappropriate and suggestive persona.

The mental condition that usually develops in adolescent phase, goes on to become a serious ailment if not checked on time and impacts the individual and the society at large.

HPD's are prone to emotional overreaction in a wide variety of situations, and as observed are constantly on edge. Their reaction to events or people is usually from a self-centered perspective, and the needs of others are seldom their priority.

They resort to manipulation and exaggerated display of emotions to steal thunder from just everyone. They scheme devious plans in their professional and personal lives to get the better of others. Not limiting their urge of attention seeking desire, finds them using emotions to misconstrue situations, dupe people and damage relationships. They are categorized as fun loving, lively and charismatic individuals who underneath is the self centered individual, devoid of empathy and someone who is carving his way to success on behest of manipulation.

The symptoms of HPD is challenging to identify as it is the degree that defines it as a disorder. It is believed that unless an individual showcases five or more of the repetitive patten it would not be deemed as HPD.

- Self-centeredness, feeling uncomfortable when not the center of attention
- Constantly seeking approval or reassurance
- Inappropriately suggestive appearance or behavior
- Rapidly shifting emotional states that appear shallow to others
- Overly inclined to physical appearance, and using physical appearance to draw attention to self
- Opinions are easily influenced by other people, but difficult to back up with details
- Excessive dramatics with exaggerated displays of emotion
- Tendency to believe that relationships are more intimate than they actually are
- Is highly suggestible (easily influenced by others)

The recommended form of treatment for histrionic personality disorder is psychotherapy but like other mental ailments it is critical to be acknowledged. While it is significant to watch our behavioral pattern it is imperative to be perceptive of others around.Base your decisions on facts instead emotions. Be careful with people who constantly pile you up with their emotional anecdotes to gain trust and eventually benefits. Practice extreme caution in saying 'Yes' to anyone or anything as your affirmation should be fact based and not an emotion based.Don't let anyone treat you as a pushover, when you were being kind to them. Will conclude with the the famous words of Paulo Coelho " When you say 'Yes' to others, make sure you are not saying 'No' to yourself"

Chapter 13

"Complexity Simplified : A Path To Excellence"

When we embark on our professional journey together, then what steers the success? Why is that some of them have touched the skies and others still in between the jobs, somehow able to survive. Is it the grades, perseverance or quintessential fate. It's the ensemble of all with a dollop of excellence in your territory. Let's delve deeper to decipher excellence, which is the differentiator. As loud as it can be, Knowledge is power. Now there are 3 levels of Knowing.

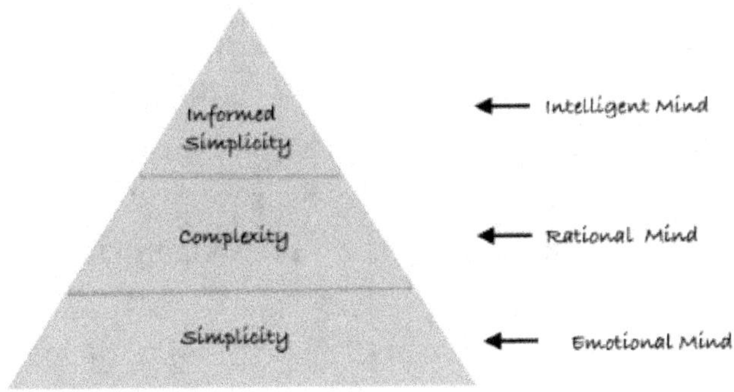

Simplicity : – The first level of elementary knowledge is from our five senses. Whatever we hear, see, feel or touch goes on to become knowledge for us, acquired in its crude form.

The **simplicity knowledge**, defines the knowledge which is not processed. It is believed that the phase is infancy, where we don't challenge the information. The manifestation of the emotional mind roots from simplicity. " I don't like the smell of fuel", "I like mountains", "I am not good with languages" are few instances wherein its largely our gut feeling or our whims which makes the decision for us.Individual in this phase tend to base their decisions on emotion and to a larger extent are unhappy with life. More often than not, their life is a rollercoaster, running on emotions. Unless the phase is outgrown, one never grows up and unfortunately ends up blaming others for things going haywire in their lives.

Complexity :- The next level of knowing information is through rationale. Challenging the elementary, attributes the **complexity information**.It is the innate quest for comprehending the obvious that drives the rational mind. Knowledge acquired from academics, world around and experience.This is the adult phase where individuals attain knowledge bu getting to the basics and unravelling the complex.The gut feeling is substituted by the rationale & logic and individual base their judgement on facts.

Emotions take a backseat for them and everything begins to add up.Grappling with complex information, data and ideas gets you success but not excellence.While the information sorted is evolved yet the sole dependence on rational mind clouds the judgement. Rationality is not the answer to all the questions, feelings being a large part of our lives.

Informed Simplicity :-The highest level of knowing information is **Informed Simplicity**. This is the phase where the complex information is simplified, processed and presented in the required form. This requires an intelligent mind which is the amalgamation of emotion and rational with intuitiveness.

This is going beyond the rudimentary form of learning. It is the proficiency and domination of the knowledge in your area which paves the way for excellence. The ability to engender the complex information in the simple form requires expertise and perseverance. As stated, "learn the trade, not the tricks of trade" that will steer to success. As matured individual, it is recommended to base your decisions on an intelligent thought with an intelligent mind.

The three levels of Knowing, is beautifully exhibited by Matthew Frederick in his book, 101 Things I Learned in Architecture School below.

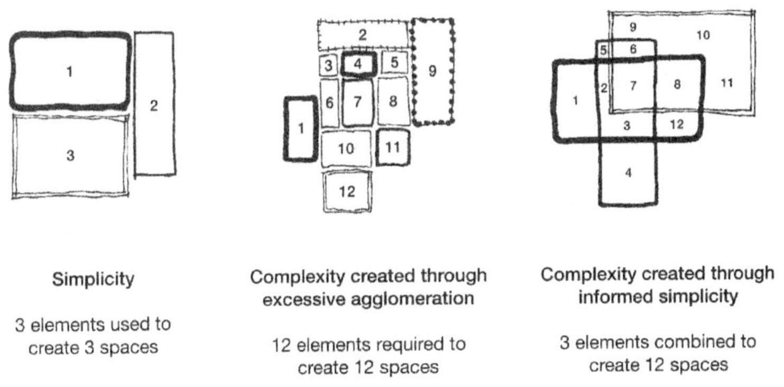

As depicted, the flow from simplicity to complexity created through informed simplicity actually said it all. This model figuratively and literally provides the crux of the variation in success and knowledge.The ability to derive complex information into simple carves the path to success. It is pertinent to excellence, success and making it big. This applies to almost all the aspects of life. Hence, master your skill and **"to become a master at any skill, it takes the total effort of your : heart, mind and soul working together in a tandem"** . If not, then the gap will augment with every passing year with the unsettling wonderment.

Chapter 14

In the words of Les Brown , **"Too many of us are not living our dreams because we are living our fears"**. For instance *"I can't leave this job even when I don't like it a bit", "I am stuck in this relationship for good", "I can never dare to travel solo"* are few of our daily fears that we are living with. Have we ever challenged our fear? or let me rephrase it, can we challenge our fear? **Absolutely!** but let's elucidate fear.

Fear is an emotion induced by any perceived threat, which causes physical, physiological and emotional changes and ultimately behavioral changes.Our reaction to stressor is a natural defense mechanism which activates under any perceived threat or danger resulting us to fleet/fight or freeze.

So the thing to ponder over is, are we born with fear? There was a study conducted bu behavioral Psychologist, John Watson along with his graduate student Rosalie Rayner at Johns Hopkins University. The premise of the study was to understand the empirical evidence of classical conditioning in humans in a controlled environment. The experiment was

conducted with a 9 year old infant, named Albert and went on to be famously called as **"The Little Albert Experiment"**.

In their experiment, Watson and Rayner exposed the little boy to a sequence of stimuli including a white rat, a rabbit, a monkey, masks, and burning newspapers to study his reactions. It was observed that initially the boy did not show any reaction to any of the stimuli.

In continuation to their experiment, when next time Albert was exposed to the white rat, Watson timed it up with the loud noise hitting a metal pipe with a hammer. But obvious, little Albert started to cry hearing the loud noise. After repeatedly pairing the white rat with the loud noise, little Albert started anticipating the loud noise whenever he saw the white rat and started to cry. It went on to an extent that soon, after seeing the rat even with no noise, little Albert would cry.

So it was furnished that emotional responses could be conditioned in humans. Though the experiment was highly criticized for its ethical base but went on to substantiate a pivotal premise. Additionally, Watson and Rayner also deduced the generalization of stimuli. For little Albert not only feared white rat but anything which resembled furry in appearance and white in color.

If we refer to the experiment and apply it to our lives, it is evident that to large extent emotional responses are conditioned in us. It can be some hapless event occurred in our childhood, abandonment, broken family or dejection. These events instill an unhappy memory in us and of our repetitive responses to them, condition it and that's how we develop fear. Fear damages us more than the damage itself. It obstructs our happiness our lives and pushes to a bigger psychological problems.

As understood, that it is conditioned so we have a scope to recreate it by challenging our fear and changing our response to it. For instance, if we have a severe stage fright then the ideal way to deal with it is to confront it. Begin with your daily fears that is making you miserable, it can be speaking in public, voicing your opinion, saying no, driving , swimming just anything.

Yes, so the next time when your fear stares at you, the best reaction is to take it head-on. Its only when you **"face your fear"** you rewire your mental programming for betterment and pave your way for contentment. In the end, we would regret the chances that we did not take, so dare to live your dream. Concluding with a famous adage, **"take care to get what you like or you will be forced to like what you get"**

Chapter 15

A maxim – *"Don't stress over something you can't change"* Yet ,"tensed before a critical match, anxious during a job interview or getting overly strained over an unpleasant news" are some of the common sight discerned by all of us. Having bouts of anxiety over stressors, is a natural defense mechanism to any perceived threat or danger and is part of (flight/flight) innate physiological reaction.

Consequently if sensed any threat, the brain responds to a threat or danger by releasing stress hormones such as adrenaline and cortisol and they cause the physical symptoms of anxiety. Once the danger or threat ceases, the physiological reactions gets back to normal. So when and how does it become a disorder?

It's when the feeling of anxiety-stress extends over a period of time and start to interfere your personal and professional life, that's when it over steps the territory of normal anxiety. This mental condition entails constant state of tension, worrying about anything and everything to an extent of breaking down. It also leads to physical ailments such as high blood pressure and nausea.

Identifying the symptoms is pivotal, to keep it at bay. The commonality in the anxiety disorder is the feeling of the below emotions over a prolonged period of time

- recurring irrational thoughts
- over-scrutinizing trivial matters
- extreme difficulty focussing
- intense feelings of dread, panic or 'impending doom'
- feeling irritable
- heightened alertness
- problems with sleep
- changes in appetite
- dissociation

The Anxiety disorder can be caused due to the combination of factors, for instance biological (genetics), environmental or through unpleasant experiences. However it can not be decided basis one or two symptoms.

Unless the condition is identified at an early stage it naturally progresses to a severe stage.

Therefore the reason it needs to be addressed is because of the nature of the disorder and how it requires self help to be treated.

The most recommended treatment for anxiety falls into two categories: psychotherapy and medication. It largely depends upon the severity level of the ailment however if it is a low or mild disorder then it is advocated to treat it through natural remedies or self help which is primarily introducing some lifestyle changes.The most effective being, meditation, getting proper sleep, balanced diet, staying active and abstaining from alcohol/smoke/caffeine. The inception of more or less all the disorder is stress, wish we could erase it. A thought,

"Don't stress the could haves, if it should have, it would have".. PERIOD.

Chapter 16

"Know Your IKIGAI aka Your Purpose In Life"

"Do what you'll love, and you'll never work another day in your life." affirms the significance of happiness in our lives. This also indicates to make the choices wisely, so that we make our way for contentment and happiness to steer us in our lives.A path towards our purpose in life, or to our calling.Now the elephant in the room is, how do we identify our purpose in life or our calling? As what gives us joy, ain't sustainable and vice versa. **IKIGAI** is the answer to it.Everybody should find their IKIGAI and if they are able to, it brings purpose to their lives and shapes it. What is IKIGAI?

IKIGAI is a Japanese concept which goes back to the Heian period (794 to 1185) and is a combination of the Japanese words **"IKI"** which translates to "life," and **"GAI"** which is used to describe value or worth, IKIGAI is all about finding happiness in life through purpose. It is popularly simplified as, your IKIGAI is what gets you up every morning and keeps you going.The principle is encapsulated in the IKIGAI venn diagram which overlaps the four primary pillars of life — **what you are good at, what the world needs, what you can be paid for, and what you love.**

It's within the crossover of these points where IKIGAI stands.It is more than just passion but a combination of the four elements that promises happiness and longevity. More often than not, we tend to find purpose in our lives through, any of the one pillar and eventually gets worn off.

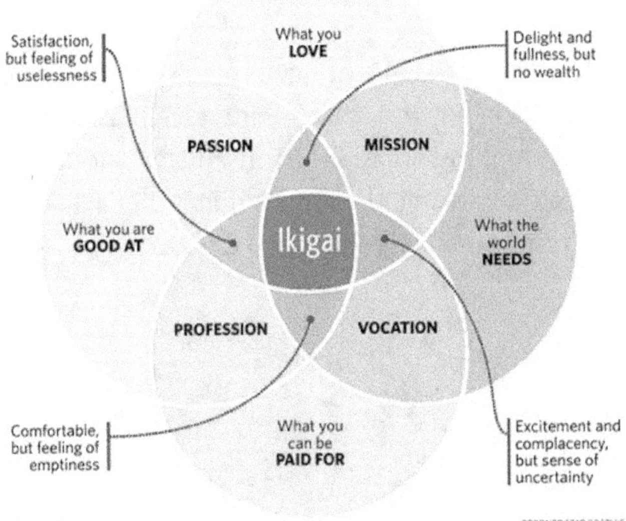

Many psychologist and scientist strongly believe in the phenomenon and have linked longevity with IKIGAI.Garcia and Miralles in their book,IKIGAI outlines it as 'the happiness of always being busy " and cited Okinawa as one place where IKIGAI is largely practiced. Okinawa is the southern island off of mainland Japan and is home to one of the highest ratios of centenarians to population. Here the mild weather, healthy diet, and low level of stress are also factors, but it's the island's active population of non-retiring, purpose-driven residents that sets them apart.

In addition to the direction that IKIGAI brings to our lives, it also directs us to be in a constant state of fluidity.. yes oxymoron it is however fluidity in terms of physical, mental and emotional keeps you light in totality.In not only chalking out the purpose in life, IKIGAI principles can be used in our daily lives wherein it can effectively help in prioritizing our long list of tasks.

Having said that, our purpose in life cannot be restricted to our profession, it goes beyond that. Your IKIGAI can be writing, painting or making someone smile but it should be naturally defined, considering the four pillars. Let's take a step towards our happiness, let's find our **IKIGAI.**

Chapter 17

"Make Peace With Your Past !!!"

We all have got past through, the dark patch in our lives. Usually we tend to forget it or harbor it deep within, to make our way forward. But do we ever get out of it ? Nope !! Our fears are manifested in our behaviors which we are oblivious off. The repression of the incident / event along with the emotion is permanently etched in our subconscious mind. Inadvertently our repressed emotion impacts our behaviour and we nurture our fear all life long.

Getting extremely self conscious, nervous around stranger, fidgety in public, distrust, volatile, violent, depressed are some the behavior that we tend to develop and when it goes unattended, it takes a form of serious condition.

The impression of our dark past lasts till the time we don't challenge it. The damage is not limited to behavior change but it influences the physiological and mental state as well. Distorted Personality is a bigger price to pay for our fears.

Hence it is imperative to acknowledge our fears in the first place. However before we embark on the path of introspection, understanding the connect and how the brain works is pivotal. The famed psychoanalyst Sigmund Freud crystallized the concept with Iceberg Model, taking the functioning of the mind analogy to iceberg.

It is Freud's premise that within the human mind is contained in three levels of awareness or consciousness which are **Conscious, Subconscious and Unconscious.**

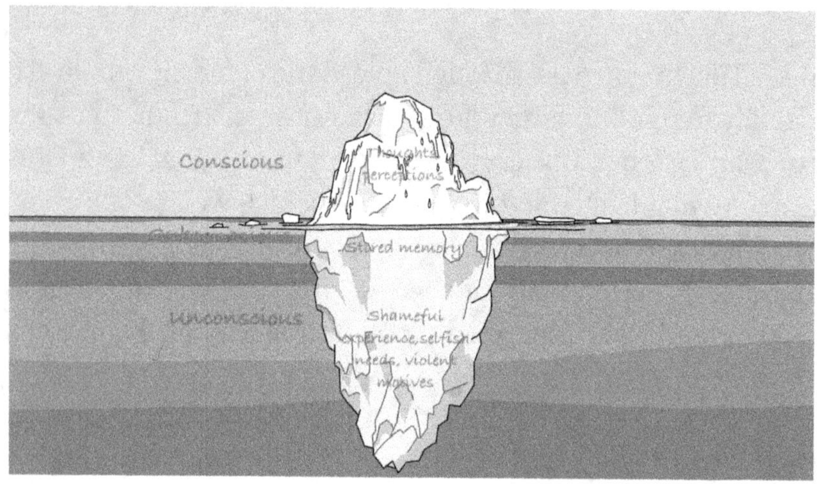

Conscious :- On the surface is conscious level that exists just below the surface of the water, which consists of those thoughts that are the focus of our attention now, and this is seen as the tip of the iceberg.Our thoughts, perception, memory and wishes which we are aware at any given point in time.

This is the aspect of our mental processing that we can think and talk about in a rational way as when required. It is somewhat akin to short-term memory and is limited in terms of capacity so 10% of your mind operates at conscious level.

Subconscious :-Next level is the subconscious or preconscious level where all the memories are stored and can be brought to the conscious level when required.

While we do not walk around consciously thinking about this information all the time, but we can quickly draw it out of your subconscious when asked to produce. For instance, if asked the model number for the first vehicle or you school teacher's name you can produce it after some recollection.The subconscious mind often dabbles with conscious mind when needed.

Unconscious :-The bottom layer which is wide ranging is the unconscious level of our mind similar to bottom of the iceberg. It acts as a repository of our primitive thoughts and impulse kept at bay and mediated by the preconscious mind. The incidents, events and desires that are often too frightening or painful for people to acknowledge are locked away in the unconscious mind.

This is usually done through repression. The ulterior motives , selfish needs, violent motives and urges , shameful experiences all the contents that are unacceptable or unpleasant are locked in the repository.

It is our unconscious mind which beholds our personality in the perspective it is formed. The intent and the endeavor is to bring the unconscious to the conscious level so that we are operating without fears. This is how we make peace with our past.The unconscious mind paves the personality and keeps interfering if not tended to.We all should strive to break-free from our past.Let's embrace our new self the one which devoid of the scars. **"I want to break Free"** in the true sense.

Chapter 18

"The Pygmalion Effect..."

"Treat people as if they were what they ought to be, and you will help them become what they are capable of becoming" ..Von Goethe might be condensing the The Pygmalion Effect....

The maxim crystalizes the concept that expectation carves the self fulfilling prophecies.We all have experienced that the teachers' expectations about individual children become self-fulfilling prophecies for instance If a teacher believes a child is intelligent, the child will come to believe that and on the contrary if the teacher believes a child is slow, the child will come to believe that, too, and will indeed learn slowly.This holds true just everywhere and has been confirmed so many times, and in such varied settings, that it's no longer even debated.The framework is called **The Pygmalion Effect.**

The Pygmalion Effect also known as the Rosenthal Effect is the phenomenon whereby higher expectations lead to an increase in performance ,named after the Ovidius tale of a sculptor who falls in love with one of his statues. To elaborate it, the name "Pygmalion" comes from the story of Pygmalion, a mythical Greek Sculptor Pygmalion carved a statue of a woman and then became enamored with it. Unable to love a human, Pygmalion appealed to Aphrodite, the goddess of love. She took pity and brought the statue to life. The couple married and went on to have a daughter named Paphos. As elucidated ,the positive expectation leads to increased performance similarly, low expectations lead to decreased performance called as the **Golem Effect.**

Both effects come under the category of self-fulfilling prophecies

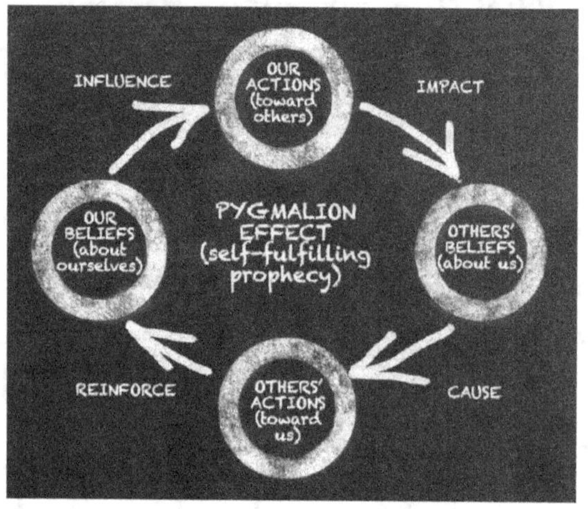

The concept exhibits in the pictorial representation, how our action towards others influences their behaviour towards us.Understanding the Pygmalion effect is a powerful way to positively affect those around us, from our children and friends to employees and leaders. For instance, If you receive frequent recognition from your boss, you are likely to feel motivated and will tend to achieve an even better performance.On the contrary, if you are continuously questioned and your work is ruthlessly criticized, the quality of your work can suffer.Hence If you expect the best in others, constructive criticism doesn't have to sound like barb or jibe. Consequently if we don't take into account the ramifications of our expectations, we may miss out on the fair benefits of holding high standards.

The Pygmalion effect is an interpersonal motivational phenomenon promising a high and positive turn around.It is important for us to understand how expectations impact our behavior and our subsequent outcomes so that we can properly mediate those expectations for the best possible outcomes.However, we also need to ensure that we don't let our expectations of particular individuals overshadow other people that may have as much to offer.

The Pygmalion effect leads to desirable outcomes for those individuals which are labelled as having high potential. If we are in a leadership position, like teachers, bosses, and therapists are, we should always maintain and express positive expectations because these expectations will actually impact how we treat those that we are supporting, as well as how those individuals behave. Consequently it leads on to a strong message, not only we are responsible for our actions but we are also responsible for other's reaction.So raise the expectation and set the bar high for all around and contribute in making top performers.

Chapter 19

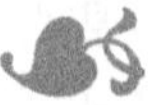

" Change your tomorrow by changing your thoughts today !!!s "

A Maxim by Henry Ford, "Whether You Think You Can, or Think You Can't ... You're Right". Actually it all starts with a thought. Your thoughts lead to emotions and eventually action. There is an innate linkage between thought, emotion and action which manifests your personality and all your achievement. This is beautifully captured in the **Cognitive triangle** as depicted pictorially , wherein what we think affects how we feel and act is at the apex of the triangle stating the significance of the thoughts.

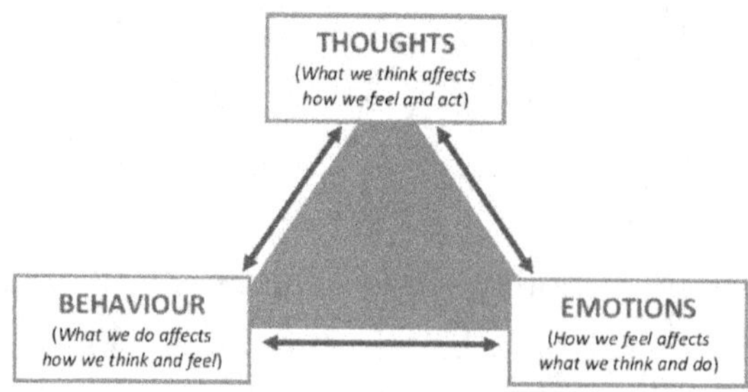

If you reflect on your lives, your would relate to this fact easily.Hence what you focus on makes you feel what you want, extending a desired or not so desired outcome. For instance, if you like a particular sport then playing it will make you happy and you might end up being a sports person.

Similarly a negative thought drives a negative action.It is imperative that we invest ourselves in creating the quality of thought.For instance, if two of your friends are working on a project together while having fun,You feel left out and a thought creeps in, *they are avoiding me as they don't like me..I am not good enough..this happens at home as well... everyone avoids me ..I am not good ...I am so miserable.*

This catastrophizing thought spiral can lead to some uncomfortable emotions that may include anxiety, worry, sadness, anger, fear, or frustration.

When we experience those feelings, we may then unintentionally play into and reinforce our negative thoughts. Consequently, with passage of time our thoughts starts to get influenced with our life events and we base our decisions on emotions or facts.

Since each of us responds to our life events differently hence we have a different outcome to same situation. Basing our decision purely on emotions is catastrophic.It is inconsistent and dwindles between good/bad. The classic example is personal relationships where emotion out rules just everything.We tend to react to our partner on an incident basis.She does good, you think good of her, she does bad and you have doubts about her.Unless you have facts to substantiate the thought we should refrain ourselves in making emotion based decision. Ideally we should strive for the fact based thought which is closer to reality. The surreal thoughts, no matter how pleased are you with it, it fades away.

Deciphering the action that we take to out thought, empower us. We can recreate the outcome bu merely changing our thought. Rightly quoted, " our quality of thought decide the quality of our life".

We should not limit our mindfulness in generating quality thoughts about ourselves but also while making a perception about others. Generating a negative perception about others tends to sabotage our peace of mind and needless to say pollutes our thought. There are three levels of perception – Thea, Theorer and Horao

Thea :- The basic level of perception is when we judge others basis the appearance.This is also termed as mindless observation which is unconsidered and we perceive on merely physical sight. This is largely practiced but fatal in nature.

Theorer :- The next level is to to make a perception of what you see at the same time explaining it to yourself. It happens when you reason it out with your logic or substantiate it with your logic.This is a modified form of Thea. However the perception is still prejudiced as it is based on your thoughts and justifications. High possibility, you may end up eating your words.

Horao :- The evolved state is Horao which is perception based without any prejudices and right from the conscious. The minute we attach our thoughts, reasoning or logic to it, it losses the essence and becomes tainted or your version.
Thought and Perception are the powerhouse and has the immense ability to change the course.So we all of us have the power to change our behavior simply by adjusting what we think. So*"Change your tomorrow by changing your thoughts today "*

Chapter 20

"Learn To Escape The Dreaded Drama Triangle !!!"

Conflicts are an intrinsic part of our lives, personal or professional, it's seldom that we can escape it. All the conflicts that we find ourselves pulled into, if observed keenly, we would notice a pattern – the three varied characteristics of a Rescuer, Victim or Persecutor that we depict or the other parties involved in display unconsciously.The three roles are interchangeable in a conflict and manifests the stance of an individual also named as **The Drama Triangle**

The drama triangle also called as the **victim triangle** was developed as a social model in 1968 by a psychologist named Stephen Karpman. Karpman's drama triangle is a dynamic framework to understand the dysfunctional roles we take on to deal with the conflict.

The three roles of the drama triangle are archetypal and easily recognizable in oneself or in others. These three types are our state of mind, representing our behaviour and thought process while we are dealing with differences of opinion or disagreements with our own self or other.Karpman placed these three roles on an inverted triangle and referred to them as being the three aspects, or faces of drama.

The Rescuer :- "*Let me help you*" is the stance of a rescuer. Karpman defines a rescuer to be striving to solve a victim's problems but matter of fact, does so in ways that result in the victim having less power, with the rescuer benefiting more than the victim. Here the rescuer is helping his innate desire of feeling valued and powerful by shifting the focus from his personal problems of his distorted personality, probably his anxiety or stress. Momentarily, the rescuer and the victim feels elated, for rescuer has helped the victim out of the situation but in reality, both of them are subjected to dysfunctional characters and bonded to their fears.

The Victim :- "*Help me, poor me*" is the stance of the victim.The victim in Karpman's triangle is not an actual victim, but rather someone feeling or acting like a victim. It has been observed that people tend to depict themselves as victim for their benefit and convenience and end up playing the role through out their lives. The feeling of being victimized by a person or a situation makes them build an external dependency beyond their reach.Conveniently, they hand over the baton of their lives to others so lack of authority and willingness to take charge of their own life and its circumstances makes them rely on others to solve their problems and in turn they have the struggle free life.

The Persecutor :- *"It's all your fault"* is the stance of the persecutor. Persecutors criticize and blame the victim, set strict limits, can be controlling, rigid, authoritative, angry and unpleasant. They call out and criticize but they don't actually solve any problems or help anyone else solve the problem. Additionally they put on a grandiose act in an attempt to hide their fear of failure and get defensive when things do not work out the way they anticipated. They seek rescue by highlighting problems and directing others as the primary cause of those problems. The validation of their beliefs come from seeking a victim (situation or a person) to hold accountable for their problems and trying to manipulate them in working their way.

It is imperative to break the drama triangle and own responsibility as this vicious triangle engulfs our self esteem and paralyzes our personality for good. Actually our nature and nurture play a huge role in determining how we manage conflicts and whether or not we choose to participate in the drama as a means to resolve the conflict. So understanding oneself is utmost important as self awareness enables us to step back and visualize others and self – our self paradigm which is the basis of paradigm of effectiveness. Then we can initiate to take accountability of ourselves and our social and professional transactions. We can also be vigilant and mindful of not being dragged in by others in any conflict.Remember we always have a choice to contribute or impede in any conflict or any situation.What is important is to enable and empower yourself as it boosts your self esteem.

Chapter 21

"Your Morality Can Be Your Biggest Limitation !!!"

Your friend is in dire need of a job and you happen to pitch him for a role in your organization for which he is not at all suited for.Out of moral obligation to him, you even go lengths to maneuver the hiring manager and get him a job. Alternately your friend confides in you of cheating the organization with their intellectual property, and you are torn in between divulging the information to the authority or supporting your friend out of moral obligation.Are one of a kind of instances where we are stuck in moral dilemmas and our morality influences our decision. We naturally succumb to our emotional discernment and outweigh morality over rationality.

Ever wondered, is it the right thing to do?

Morality, largely defines itself as principles concerning the distinction between right and wrong or good and bad behaviour.However this is not it, morality is beyond right or wrong.

"With age comes wisdom," declared Oscar Wilde. *"But sometimes age comes alone."*

Analogously morality comes with age.Jean Piaget introduced the idea of how moral development occurs in stages, each level built on life experiences and active reasoning.

Lawrence Kohlberg in 1958 furthered this idea by examining how moral reasoning transitions as we grow. He organized the six stages into three levels of moral reasoning post his experiment with using boys only as his subject.The three broad levels are **Pre-Conventional, Conventional and Post- Conventional.**

Pre Conventional :- The pre-conventional level of moral reasoning is mostly observed in children aged below nine, although adults can also exhibit this level of reasoning. Individuals in the pre-conventional level judge the morality of an action by its direct consequences. At this stage, according to Kohlberg, people see rules as fixed and absolute and they adhere to it as a means to avoid punishment.

The pre-conventional level further consists of two stages:

Stage 1: Punishment/obedience orientation

Individuals are driven by the consequences of their actions.At young age, children reason out their actions resulting to punishment so avoids it. If they have been reprimanded for being late, they would be obedient and will be on time.Harder the punishment, higher the adherence.

Stage 2: Instrumental purpose orientation- At this stage, children seeks personal benefit as a sole reason for their moral reasoning.They realize the fact that with every transaction they can negotiate and look for themselves in it.Hence children seek rewards in exchange of adhering to dictum laid down by their parents.

This stage is termed as pre-conventional due to the limited association that children have with the outlined principles. They perceive the ethics taught as something that society imposes, not as something they internalize themselves and with their limited cerebral development opts for either obedience or reward.

Conventional :- The conventional level of moral reasoning is archetypal of adolescents and teenagers were conforming to societal views and expectations is the driving force.The emphasis shifts from self-interest as in Pre Conventional, to relationships with other people and social systems. Children, mostly pre teen or teens strives to support rules that are set forth by others such as parents, peers, and the authorities in order to win their approval or to maintain social order.

Stage 3: Good Boy/Nice Girl orientation – The stage three is primarily of carrying good image which gets them a social nod or an acceptance by sticking to what is considered to be right as instructed by parents, peers or authorities.

Stage 4: Law and order orientation – Moral reasoning in stage four is thus beyond the need for individual approval exhibited in stage three.A this stage, teenager acknowledges the fact that it is important to obey laws, dictums and social conventions because of their importance in maintaining a functioning society.

Post Conventional :- At the post- conventional level, the individual moves beyond the perspective of societal norms or law &order and reasons out through abstract principles and values that apply to all situations and societies. The individual attempts to take the perspective of all individuals.At this evolved level, adult realizes that rules are not absolute dictates that must be obeyed without question.It can be challenged hence it is at this stage that individuals elevate their own moral evaluation of a situation over social conventions.

Stage 5: Social contract orientation – At stage five, individuals tend to deliberate on the morals and ethics of the society and identifies the disconnect in their personal values and attempts to fix what they do not conform with. It is at this matured stage when individuals accept the fact of others holding different opinions and values, and it is paramount that they be respected and honored impartially. Thats where the whole unity in diversity stems from.

Stage 6: Universal ethical principle orientation – According to Kohlberg, this is the highest stage of functioning wherein the appropriate action is determined by one's self-imbibed ethical principles based on conscience.This is the most evolved stage where individuals follow the internalized principles of justice, even if they conflict with laws and rules.

A common observation is that individual seldom reaches to stage five or six but is subconsciously pinned at level one or two.

As cited by Kohlberg and Piaget, individual should have their moral conscious evolved with age. It is because of our inability to outgrow our moral reasoning that we base our decisions on pleasing others life long, by seeking reward, avoiding punishment or conforming to something that we are not aligned with. Ideally as matured individuals we should strive to upscale our moral conscious with developing a personal code of behaviour which is not tainted with the varied levels of moral development as stated..

Chapter 22

"Your Choices Defines You ..."

"Every uncomfortable experience in life gives you the option of growing bitter or better" maxim by Orrin Woodward crystallizes the basis, for the person that we are today. It goes back to the time when we were infant, heavily reliant on others for our basic needs. Since then we have been harboring the learnings that we deduced out of every experience and eventually these learnings contribute in shaping our personality.However at every adverse incident, we are faced with two conflicting choices and it is the one we opts makes the difference.

A famous anecdote, wherein two brothers with tremendous troubled childhood grew up to be with diametrically opposite personality. When questioned, both had different stances on their experience and the choice that they made. One of them wanted to change the situation and the other merely relived it. Crux is, the choices that we make, carves the person that we are today. **Erikson's Stages of Psychosocial Development**, a theory introduced in the 1950s by the psychologist and psychoanalyst Erik Erikson echoes the principle.

According to Erikson, ego makes positive contributions to development by reconciling the conflicting states at each stage of development.He defined eight stages to psychosocial development wherein these eight sequential stages of human development influenced by biological, psychological, and social factors throughout the lifespan complements the psychosocial development.

Each stage is defined by two opposing psychological tendencies one positive and negative. From this stems an ego virtue/strength or maldevelopment, respectively. If the virtue is adopted, it can help to resolve the current decision and prepares for the subsequent stages of development while contributing to a stable foundation for core belief systems. The eight stages as depicted in the below exhibit, expands throughout the human lifespan from infancy to adolescence and maturity.

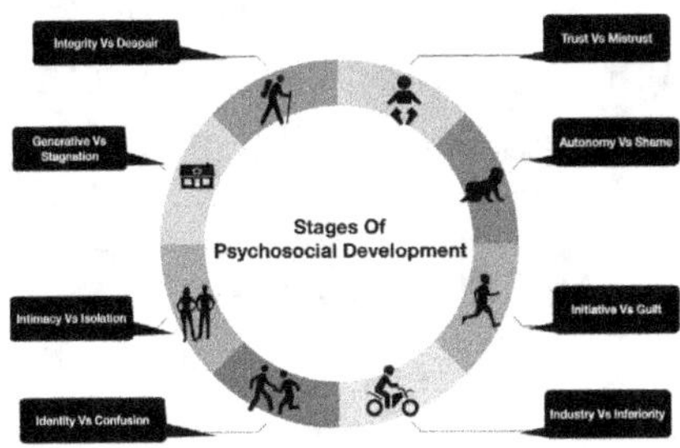

Stage 1 :- Infancy period: Trust vs. Mistrust – The first stage occurs between birth and until 1 year of age and is considered to be the fundamental stage in life.It is in this period that a child learns to trust/mistrust basis the experience he has. For instance, as an infant a child is utterly reliant on the caregivers for food, love, nurturing, just everything. If the caregiver is able to cater to all his needs reliantly, the child learns to trust, instead if the caregiver falters, then unknowingly the mistrust is instilled in the child for good.

Stage 2 :- Early Childhood period: Autonomy vs. Shame – The second stage of Erikson's theory of psychosocial development takes place during early childhood and is focused on children developing a greater sense of personal control. By encouraging the kids to make personal choices in the little things that they do, instills autonomy and failing to give them that independence contributes a deeper self doubt or inadequacy in them.

Stage 3 – Pre School period : Initiative vs. Guilt – At this stage in psychosocial development, children begin to assert their power and control over the people or situation around them.If supported in their initiatives or decisions they learn to be confident of themselves otherwise with their initiative misfiring or stifled by over-controlling parents the guilt seeps in them creating a deep dent in their confidence.

Stage 4 – School Age period: Industry vs. Inferiority – At stage four of psychosocial development children begin to develop a sense of pride in their accomplishments and abilities in school or at social events. Children who are commended by parents and teachers develop a feeling of competence and belief in their skills however those who receive little or no encouragement from parents or teachers, doubt their abilities and grow up to feel inadequate or inferior.

Stage 5 – Adolescence period: Identity vs. Identity confusion – The fifth stage of Erik Erikson's theory of psychosocial development is identity vs. role confusion, and it occurs during adolescence. This is the critical stage where adolescents explore their self and under proper encouragement and reinforcement will emerge with a strong sense of self belief and feelings of independence and control. On the contrary the less encouraged teens gets more confused and harbor more self doubt of themselves and their future.

Stage 6 – Young Adulthood period: Intimacy vs. Isolation – At this stage of early adulthood, individuals are faced with intimacy or isolation. After developing a sense of self belief in adolescence, they are ready to share their life with others. If by now, the individuals have developed a low esteem or sense of inadequacy they will have trouble developing and maintaining successful relationships with others. Erikson emphasizes that we must have a strong sense of self before we can develop successful intimate relationships. Adults who do not develop a positive self belief in adolescence may experience feelings of loneliness and emotional isolation.

Stage 7 – Adulthood period: Generativity vs. Stagnation – Generativity versus stagnation is the seventh of eight stages of Erik Erikson's theory of psychosocial development. This stage takes place during middle adulthood.Through generativity we develop a sense of being a part of the bigger picture as bi this time we are through with our responsibilities of raising our children, being evolved at work, and becoming involved in community activities and organizations.Being successful leads to feelings of usefulness and accomplishment, while failure results in sense of unwanted and unproductive.

Stage 8 – Old Age period: Integrity vs. Despair – The old age period from the mid-60s to the end of life, we are in the period of development known as late adulthood. At this stage we reflect on our lives and feel either a sense of pride or a sense of failure. People who feel proud of their accomplishments feel a sense of integrity however, people who are not successful at this stage may feel as if their life has been wasted. They deliberate on their lives and have regrets which brings in the them the sense of bitterness, depression, and despair.

The interesting fact with Erickson's model is that the outcome at every sequential stage becomes fixed if not addressed when the next stage is engaged.

So it is imperative that we deliberate on the two conflicting forces at every stage of our lives and reconcile with them to emerge out as balanced individual. As much as we like to be on the positive end of the spectrum the mere fact of us being human brings us in the middle of it where we tend to have alternating states at any given point in time.What is important is to factor the positive state and develop a strong self worth.

It is our self worth which directs us to make reasonable choices and brings out the best in us.

Hence it can be inferred that, **we choose our joys and sorrows long before we experience them" – Kahlil Gibran**

Chapter 23

" Projection (Blaming others) is self destruction "

I remember a funny incident from the past, wherein my year old niece ate some candies in spite of being told otherwise. On being questioned, she innocently told us, that her teddybear pushed her into eating the candies. Now after years to that incident, on deliberation, I discern how as an adult we still practice projection so seriously in our daily lives. Projecting onto others has become an acceptable norm.

So what is Projection? it is defined as a defense mechanism in which the ego defends itself against unconscious impulses or qualities by denying their existence in themselves and by attributing them to others, events or environment.Projecting is an innate characteristic of a personality disorder named **Narcissistic Personality Disorder (NPD)**.They are also called blamers.

Blamers are all around and can come in all the different forms, a friend of yours who has never grown out of his mishap happened in childhood, a cousin of yours who is self absorbed, an office colleague who has a sob story to avoid doing his work or overly critical family member. No matter who they are, but this kind of person single-handedly dents your happy self, damages your confidence with their remark, twists your good news into bad news in seconds, make a happy, person depressed, and they generally just make life miserable of everyone around.

They have aversion to other's happiness and instantly turn it into bad atmosphere by their biting remarks.One of my senior office colleague has this scathing habit of demeaning people and spoiling their moment with her biting remarks. For instance, if anyone wears a new attire, she would touch the fabric and comment, I had the same dress, better quality and expensive which I gave it to the maid.

This behaviour is toxic and dealing with such people is nothing less than harassment.
As a society at large, we have embraced projection (blaming)

to an extent that blamers conveniently shirk their responsibilities onto others and steers on into damaging others. It is imperative that we identify blamers and strive to stand up against their atrocities.

How to identify blamers

- Blamers never take responsibility of their actions whatsoever
- They have aversion to change and likes to be in control
- They are self absorbed and can never think beyond themselves. Their needs are of utmost importance and that's how they like people around them to believe it.
- They usually have nothing good to say about others and are super critical. Their cheap thrill is destroying other's moments
- Their actions can be deemed as immature and shortsighted
- They have this distinguish characteristic of exaggerating their success or failure. It is always one big story they have that beats everyone's experience.
- They always have their way in just everything and it usually involves manipulation, scheming or emotional exploitation.
- For them every relationship is a means to their ends, completely oblivious of other's sentiments.
- They have this innate belief of never being wrong and it's impossible for them to accept their mistakes
- Importantly, every interaction with them makes you feel awful or leaves a bad taste in your mouth
- Another thing, their self high handedness would never let you challenge them. They are equipped to deal

with emotions for their benefit and will more often than not, will use them to instill guilt.

It is absolute unfortunate to be subjected to one.But again, we hardly have control to it however we can incorporate mechanisms to alleviate the impact.

How to deal with blamers

- When dealing with blamers, ensure that you are using your rational mind compared to emotional mind. Meaning, you have to keep a check on your emotions and rationalize their actions vis a vis your actions.
- Never take a blamer on their face value. Accept the fact that "what you see is not what you get". They always fall short of fulfilling their tall claims of being around. Hence never trust them
- Refrain yourself from getting into an argument, explanation or being defensive with blamers and avoid confronting them as they will devoid you of your peace of mind.
- Acknowledge their personality disorder and don't let them influence you in anyway. Limit your interaction to minimal and nurse yourself when hurled with scathing remarks. Remember they need help not you so keep your self esteem intact.
- Avoid giving suggestions/advice to them as sooner or later you would be blamed for the repercussions.
- Lastly, never trust them. They can go to lengths to prove themselves right or to retaliate with an intention of destroying you.

Concluding with the famous words of Robert Kioysaki, ***"When people are lame they love to blame"***.

Understand, there is a reason why it is called a personality disorder and is recommended for help. The little we can do is to acknowledge and educate people so that they don't get victimized by any blamer.

Chapter 24

As a human we all undergo setbacks / loses all through our lives, of which some are grave as in bereavement, terminal illness and others minor as in losing a job or financial loss. It is believed that these setbacks – chain of events are instrumental in carving the personality. Ever wondered, How do we react to these turn of events? Astonishingly, there is a definitive pattern of reactions that we all experience and exhibit while we are subjected to any mishap.

A response by human to such situations is explained by a Swiss- American psychiatric Elisabeth Kubler Ross who developed a model which is also widely known **Kubler-Ross Change Curve or 5 Stages of Grief and Loss.**

Kubler-Ross researched on the subject of bereavement and experience of dying and came up with 5 Stages of Grief and Loss which was published in her book in 1969 titled Death and Dying. These five stages represent a series of emotions a person goes through after experiencing traumatic situation. The stages, popularly known by the acronym **DABDA** is shown in the below exhibit.

THE CHANGE CURVE

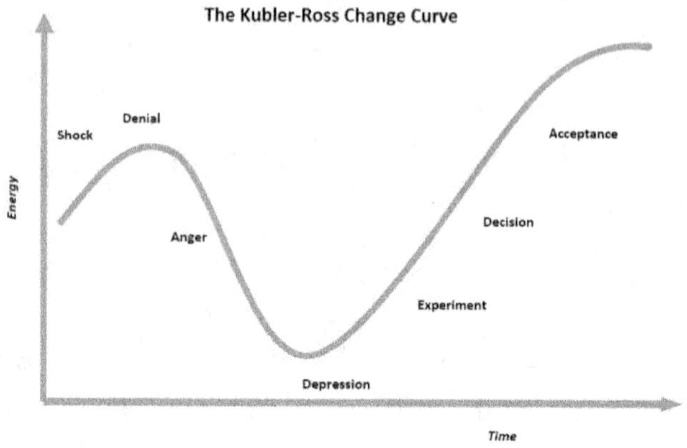

Denial – The first reaction to any mishap is denial with is a temporary defense where individuals refuse to accept and takes time to absorb the news. It is the initial stage of numbness and shock. We don't want to believe that it is happening.Exasperated phrases like "I can't believe it", "This can't be happening", "Not to me!", "Not again!" does the rounds.

• **Anger** – The second stage is when the event seeps in and that's when denial usually turns to anger. The anger is subjected towards proximate individuals and questions like "Why me? It's not fair!"; "How can this happen to me?"; "Who is to blame?"; "Why would this happen?" starts to surface out.It is observed that the anger can be directed in the directions where we perceive to have been originated from. For instance, if it is a loss of job then towards the organization, if it is a bereavement then towards God or if duped then it can be towards themselves.

- **Bargaining** – The third stage is a phase where the individual tries to make sense of what is happening. When the stage of anger is past us, we start to think about ways to postpone the inevitable and try to find out the best thing left in the situation. Those who are not faced by bereavement but by another traumatic situation may try to negotiate in the situation and come to a point of compromise. The search for a different outcome or a less traumatic one may remain on during this stage. This is the phase of trying hard to hold on to the remnants by negotiating secret deals with God, others, or life, where we say "please God do this and I will mend my ways" or "we cannot be together but we can be friends", "please God I will study hard if I pass this test"

- **Depression** – The fourth stage is often noticeable wherein the individual may become silent, refuse visitors and spend much of the time mourning or nursing the grief.In this phase individuals completely give up as they are now fully aware of the losses and their life without it. They can witness what has been left behind and how it is to be moving forward.This is the lowest point in the emotional journey and individual realizes that **This Is It** and there is no turning back.

- **Acceptance** – As people realize that fighting the unhappy occurrence is not going to make it go away they move into a stage of **acceptance**.It is not a happy space, but rather a resigned attitude towards the change so they resign to the situation and accept it completely. Phrases like "It's going to be okay."; "I can't fight it; I may as well prepare for it" starts to build up which usually is a positive mark as it propels you forward.

In the Change Curve model, Elisabeth Kübler-Ross considered these stages, not as a linear process, but rather observed these could be gone through in random order wherein individuals can jump backwards and repeat stages too. The objective is to reach the acceptance stage to any unforeseen event.

The emotional journey from the time the information was released until it was consumed is pretty standard and this is the fundamental reason that the reaction is manifested in various forms to cope with change. This change model is popularly practiced by corporates while introducing any changes in the organization and is considered to be a powerful tool in change management. This tool also gives us an insight on a personal level to empathize , when dealing with a loss or someone in proximity going through a change. So we can brace up ourselves for any change as **"Change is the only constant"**.

Chapter 25

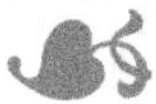

Our Beliefs contribute immensely in creating the person that we are today. It is not the event in our lives, instead it is the beliefs that cause us to experience emotions such as anger, depression or anxiety. These emotions control our actions and eventually it goes on to carve the personality. So it is imperative to seed our beliefs with rationality to be able to lead a happy life.

This concept was conceived by Albert Ellis in the 1950s. It's an approach that helps you identify irrational beliefs and negative thought patterns that may lead to emotional or behavioral issues.Now all of us want to achieve our goals and find happiness. But more often than not, irrational thoughts and feelings get in the way. These beliefs can influence how we perceive circumstances and events — usually not for the better.To elucidate the concept, let me cite an example which shall outline the **ABC model**.You went for an interview last week and did not hear from the organization. Your mind will start to feed you with thoughts like, I must have not cleared it, I was sounding desperate, I was not confident. I will be without job etc. Even if the reality is that the organization is waiting for the final go-ahead. Now here the ABC Model can be explained as

A refers to the **A**ctivating event that triggers a pessimistic response which in this case is, lack of response

B refers to the **B**eliefs or irrational thoughts that stemmed from the event which is that you will be without job.

C refers to the **C**onsequence which is the distressing emotion of worthlessness or of being good for nothing.

Usually every individual responds differently to each incidents or events making it a personality trait. So the next obvious question that creeps in is, how does the negative thoughts originate?Albert Elvis further adds on, that negative beliefs are the outcome of three commonly irrational belief Coined as the **"Three Basic Musts,"** these three common irrational beliefs are based on a stipulation – about ourselves, others, or the environment. They are

1. I must do well and it is pivotal for me to win other's approval or else I am no good.
2. Others must treat me in all fairness and be nice to me and in the same way I want them to treat me and if they fail to do so then they deserve to be punished.
3. I must get whatever I want and if I don't then I'm miserable.

In all the three must's, if it is not realized then we feel anxious, angry or self-pity in the order.Is it fair to pollute our thought process and associate it with unreasonable demands that it becomes the sole reason of our unhappiness.It is evident that we are fueling our beliefs with pessimism that it is becoming the cause of our misery.

So how do we overcome this, how do we come out of it? The answer is to challenge the irrational beliefs or dispute the unreasonable belief. It is to avoid self judgement and be more tolerant of our self. We should realize that we all are humans and we all can and all will make errors.That is why it's been said " **To err is human, to forgive is divine**".

We have to train ourselves to be more acceptable of ourselves and others.If you start to accept the reality, whether that reality is pleasant or unpleasant that will make you emotionally healthy. Emotionally healthy is the state of mind that is free from pessimistic thoughts, stress and anxiety. By imbibing the emotional healthy state, we will have rational thoughts to any event in our lives.We cannot control the outcome but we have the power to control our thoughts, belief and action.

Chapter 26

"Cognitive Distortions"

In this Pandemic, we are already amidst multiple problems such as layoff, pay-cut, hospitalization and many more. The least we can do is to stay positive and composed. It is imperative that adverse situations of such magnitude, pulls an individual down to their lowest self. It impacts their core, affecting their mental balance to an extent that the thought process gets distorted. The thoughts such as I would never get a job, I can never come out of the debt comes naturally and is called Cognitive Distortion.

Cognitive Distortion are thoughts that cause an individual to perceive reality negatively.During adverse situations, these distorted thoughts can contribute to an overall negative outlook on the world and a depressive or anxious mental state.Most people experience cognitive distortions from time to time. But if they're reinforced often enough, they can increase anxiety, deepen depression, and lead to a host of other complications. In the 1960s, psychiatrist Aaron Beck pioneered research on cognitive distortions in his development of a treatment method known as Cognitive Behavior Therapy, Researchers have identified primarily eight types of cognitive distortions.

Polarised Thinking – It means thinking that everything is Yes/No or black /white. This is a serious problem with the perfectionist. For instance, you got a gymnasium membership and is following diligently for weeks.Due to some reason you had to miss for a week and now with polarized distortion you would feel it useless to continue and would leave it.Either it is all or nothing.

Overgeneralization – This distortion manifests exaggeration and one mistake tends you to believe that nothing can go good with you.This always happens with you, based on 1-2 incidents. For instance, you are going for an interview and do it very well apparently the HR says they will get back to you. The disbelief creeps in immediately that you would not get through because it happened before as well.There is no rationale behind the thought.

Jumping To Conclusion – This "Jumping to Conclusions" distortion manifests as the inaccurate belief that we know what another person is thinking. At times we are able to figure it out but believing that you know it at all times in negative connotation is a distortion. if someone did not smile at you for reasons unknown, you are to believe that it is because of you, Anything going wrong with anyone out there, you tend to take it on yourself.

Magnification – Popularly known as the "Binocular Trick" for its stealthy skewing of your perspective, this distortion involves magnifying or minimizing the meaning, the essence or likelihood of things.For instance, as a hardworking professional you stretch yourself to keep up with the deadline of the project but a single mistake of yours delayed it. Beating yourself as the one to messed up the project is magnification.

Emotional Reasoning – Emotional reasoning refers to the acceptance of one's emotions as fact.This distortion is very common and all of us have experienced it. For instance I feel that I will not be able to crack this interview or I feel that he is lying about the incident.Feeling things without the facts cannot be true.It is a form of distortion as the belief gets so strong that eventually it starts to impact negatively.

Should Statements – Another particularly damaging distortion is the innate tendency to make "should" statements. Should statements are statements that you make to yourself about what you "should" do, or what you "must" do.It damages, when you hang on to your should statements for long. Even if it is used for others, it brings unhappiness as we cannot bound people in our should statements. In both the circumstances, when used for self or others it brings misery and loads of negative thoughts that distorts our mental capacity to think straight. For instance, I should wake up before 5am every day or she should be supporting me in everything since she is my friend.

Labelling & Mislabelling – This form of distortion is making a judgement of self or others on the basis of one odd incident. It is an extension of exaggeration of the situation wherein you tend to add value to people. For instance, if someone failed at a game then we are quick to label him/her as the person is a loser. If you could not speak up on the stage once, you concluded that you have a stage fright. It is damaging to anyone.

Personalization – As the name implies, this distortion involves taking everything personally or assigning blame to yourself without any logical reason to believe you are to blame.For instance you go to your friend's party and the party turns out into not so great, so you start to reason out how is it related to you/or it has a to do with you. You would even weave out the whole story to   make yourself responsible.

These distortions while are normal but potentially damaging to us if not addressed timely.Beck, Burns, and other researchers in this area have developed multiple ways to identify, challenge, minimize, or erase these distortions from our thinking. To start with, identifying the distortion is primary. The most recommended approach is to list down your cognitive distortion and then cataloging the events with facts. Then reason out the belief that is derived from that incident.It is a tedious exercise but very helpful to disseminate the distortions.Help yourself and if required seek help from professional. Old adage but can relate to it, **"When going gets tough, tough gets going"**

Chapter 27

" Natural Response (Fight/Flight/Freeze) "

Pulsating heartbeat, sweaty palms, dry mouth, tense muscles and dilating pupils while you encounter a beast or when called out to address the room filled with people is a common reaction to most of us in difficult situations. For some, this reaction may come out, while they pulled the vehicle after avoiding an abrupt animal which came from nowhere. But it takes little longer to come back to the normal self. We all have undergone through such physiological changes in some extremely stressful situations. Thing to ponder over is, why do we react in a particular fashion to any threat?

Back in the 1920s, a physiologist named Walter Cannon described what he called the acute stress response. It's also been called the fight or flight response. Later on, many physiologists refined his work by deliberating on the theory and came up with an understanding of flight/fight/freeze as a natural reaction to acute stress.

Flight response – When your brain signals to run away as a solution to tough situations

Fight response – When you are signaled to be able to deal with it by fighting it out

Freeze response – When your brain sends the signal to freeze

Before the fight-flight-freeze response kicks in, something happens to make you feel you're in danger. This threat may be real or perceived. Someone or something may be threatening to cause you physical or psychological harm. As soon as you recognize a threat, your nervous system shifts into the acute stress response. Either its fight/flight or freeze signal by the brain which has some definitive psychological and physiological changes. The physiological changes can be tense muscles, breathlessness, pulsating heartbeat, high blood pressure, profusely sweat etc and the psychological changes can be anxiety, stress or brain going completely blank. It is evident that the body and mind undergoes through lot of changes when kicked in with any life-threatening situations.

However, the bigger problem here, which I want to cater to is our lack of identifying the situations from life threatening and natural threat to perceived threat. In our complex world that we have built in, we are dealing with the stress frequently or on a daily basis. The stress which could stem out of missing on a deadline, missing on a delivery or getting into a tough or sticky situation of losing an opportunity or getting into conflict. Unfortunately, the brain could not differentiate between the natural or perceived threat and initiates working in the same way it does when faced with acute stress.

So, the natural defense mechanism which is meant to be activated in a really threatening situations is now being activated in every stressful situation that we perceive as threat. The physiological and psychological changes that one undergoes through on a regular basis adversely impacts the wellbeing, nudging the individual into sickness which can take any form (mental or physical).

The solution here is an absolute requirement to differentiate between the natural threat and perceived threat, the life-threatening situations or the difficult yet manageable situations. This comes with practice. You must train yourself to take things seriously when it ought to be. For mild stressful situations you must train yourself to take it lightly by defining rules as it is ok with losing an opportunity as you will make it later. You must have a positive self-talk and constant reminder of work tend to be taken as work and not your identity or being. Have confidantes, friends with whom you may discuss issues and diffuse it. Additionally, one should try practicing hard to maintain calm by meditation or any activity which helps in keeping your mind controlled. In cases when you have difficulty helping yourself then you may seek external help. The intent is to keep your priorities prioritized so that you can keep unnecessary stress at bay and live life happily, which is doable.

Chapter 28

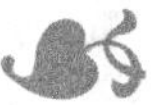

"Self Worth Vs Self Esteem"

Ever wondered why you need an approval from others for any of your decisions or why is this constant urge to please people even if that calls for sacrificing your happiness. This is because of low self worth. How do we get low self worth and how does it impact our self esteem? Self worth and self esteem, though used interchangeably however are poles apart and impacts an individual 's personality to a larger extent.

Self worth is an identity of an individual which is how he appears to himself or sees himself. That true identity of self ,holds the deeper bearing on his personality. Wherein **Self Esteem** is the outward personality of an individual perceived by the world. It is largely based on perception of the people, what they think about you. So we can conveniently deduce that self esteem stems from self worth.

Self Worth is created from the time a child is conscious of the surrounding. Kids with broken families, unhappy incidents such as bereavement , living in other's house away from parents, and poverty goes a long way to create a low self worth. Whatever made the kid felt ashamed of , laughed at, ridiculed , compared with others in a demeaning way ,all of it contributes in developing a low self worth. The feeling of unworthy or being worthless creeps in   and with every passing year the feeling takes a form of opinion and eventually an identity. Such kids grow up into a vulnerable adult , who are the ones mostly abused. The abuse can be in all the forms, mental , physical or emotional. On the contrary the kids who are loved, cherished and appreciated with the strong background grows to have a high self worth. They take pride in themselves, their work and their background. People's opinion is an opinion for them not the verdict of themselves. They can think objectively, detaching the emotion from the situation.

However with low self worth people, their strong urge of attaining acceptance by others makes them to continually work for other's happiness. Their happiness is dependent upon people's verdict. They are the "YES" man. They have a difficulty in saying NO to any thing hurled at the them. They push themselves hard to be someone else, that someone ,who is liked by all. This is a sorry state to be in as you are basing your identity on others opinion. They cannot handle rejection and mere thought of it makes then anxious to the level of extremes stress. That is when they take extreme steps.

So, what is imperative to deliberate upon is, can we come out of the low self worth and lead a happy life? The answer is affirmative. We can and we should. To begin with, it starts with acknowledgement of the problem. Once identified , we can work on our self talk. The self talk is what we say to ourselves for e.g I am not good enough, I can't do this, I am not beautiful anything. In order to get a high self worth we have to replace our negative self talk with positive self talk , for e.g I am worth it, I am good, I am beautiful, I can do this. The perpetual reminder of the positives will bring in the belief in self which will bring back the self worth. This is easy said than done. Trust me, this is worth the try. Nothing is more precious than having a true identity of self which outweighs the self esteem. You will feel free. It will make you realize that every laugh, every denial and every rejection is not because of you. There is altogether a whole lot of dynamics in getting things wrong. It will give you power, power to be in control of your happiness.

It will require a lot from people to break you and let me reiterate, Never let anyone break you and if ever you want to give in it should be with your approval. It is then that you shine back.

About the Author

Munit Vikram is a Human Resource professional, and a Self Help enthusiast by vocation. She has had an innate inclination towards helping people which acted as enablers in her mission of helping people. She is a Master Practitioner in Neuro Linguistic Programming and certified in Cognitive Behaviour and Rationale Emotive Behaviour. Over years she has helped people fight their fears and overcome their limitations to explore their full potential. She dares you to go beyond yourself by calmly touching the right chords.